LYDIA

Lydia

kenneth
gangemi

black sparrow press   los angeles   1970

SBN: 87685-007-7 (paper)
    87685-008-5 (limited cloth)

CONTENTS

LYDIA

For Antoine César Becquerel (1788-1878)

Alexandre Edmond Becquerel (1820-1891)

and Antoine Henri Becquerel (1852-1908)

CLASSROOM

Boredom

I stare at
The number 2

I stare at
The number 2

I stare at
The number 2

It looks
Like a swan!

SUMMER FARM

Orchard sunrise

Sunny brook
Sunny morning

Hampshire hogs
Black angus

Sun on soil

Horses and honeybees
Falcons and flowers

Meadow girls

Hollyhocks
Foxgloves
Buttercups
Daffodils

Summer cumulus

The smell of warm fields
The sound of a distant airplane

Orchard bluebirds

White potatoes from the black earth
Red apples from the green trees

Summer suppers

Cricket evenings

SEAPORT

Bananaboats
Sugarships

Gypsy ships
Mineral ships

Skates for Hawaii
Sugar for Alaska

Texas taxis

Cinnamon and cinnabar
Copper and cocoa

Nashville lambkins

Bullets and bibles
Violins and vodka

Fellini films

Crucificas
Swastixes

Foo dogs

Motorcycles for Mexico
Kangaroos for Kalamazoo

Yokohama kittens

Giant microscopes
Midget telescopes

African junglegyms

Metal manacles
Made in Michigan

Whorehouse hardware

Calico for Kokomo
Tampax for Tahiti

Plastic chalices

Jamaica ginger
Saigon cinnamon

Eskimos for Africa
Mexicans for Alaska

FLORIDA

Florida mornings
Gulfstream green

Green water
White sand

Green grass
Red roads

Royal palms
Coconut palms

Cypress picnics
Picnic pelicans

Pawpaws and pompanos
Cardinals in orange trees

Jasmine nights

READER

Ten-ounce heart

Bony skeleton
Largely levers

Six-hour stomach
Seven-quart lungs

Grooved tongue
Translucent cheeks

Sweat-diverting eyebrows
Insect-stopping nosehairs

Snarling muscle
Atavistic palm-pad

Vestigial tail-wagging muscle
Vestigial fur of comic proportions

15-pound head
20-watt brain

Plantigrade
Upright gait

Binocular vision
Opposable thumb

Versatile epidermis

PLEISTOCENE

Amphibious rhinoceroses!
Giant land tortoises!

Megatheriums!
Glyptodons!

Lion-like cats!
Hyenoid dogs!

Camelids!
Deerlets!

BAPTISTS

Texas Sundays

Grim grandmothers
Empty engineers

Crew cuts
Thick necks
Shiny suits

Proper people
Private property

Crosshairs on their eyeballs

Secret collections of hooks
Secret ponds of cartilaginous fishes

Gentle smiles

Rifles for the country
Pistols for the city

Mighty bibles

GUATEMALA

Quetzal!

ARCTIC WARM-UP

We are living in the spring
Of the fourth interglacial summer

Tropical Alaska

Polar palms
Polar pumpkins

Arctic Arabs

Polar picnics
Polar prostitutes

Arctic anarchists

Polar robots
Polar postcards

Arctic music

Polar parrots on polar cactus
Polar pythons in polar jungle

Tropical tundra

Arctic cocktails
Arctic architects

Visit the Alaskan Riviera

LIFE STYLE

Programmed commuters

Rushing for Train Zero
To the novocaine suburbs

Products of a culture

The right shirt
The right cocktail

Treadmill lifetimes

Shirts by the dozen
Liquor by the case

Trapped men

Each with a master
Each told what to do

Quicksand corporations

Tear off your white collars!
Throw away your class rings!

Useless

The invisible harness
The bit and blinders

Cheerful robots

FLORIDA CITIES

Coral Gables
Cocoa Beach

Gulfport

Ocala
Okeechobee

Palmetto
Pensacola

Palm Beach
Pompano Beach

Port Everglades

Sebring
Sarasota
Seminole

Tampa
Tallahassee

FUTURE

New shores
Old oceans

The Polar Express
The Amazon Express

Mars the desert planet
Venus the jungle planet

Green tropical cities
White arctic cities

Lake Sahara
Amazon City

Orchard islands
Tropical seafarms

Beach cities
Garden cities

Green nations

SPOUSE

I

Morning

Warm bed

Nuzzling the warm wife

Grain-eating female
Good-smelling skin

Soft back
Soft belly
Soft breasts

Shoulders
Sleepy hair

II

Evening

Kitchen kiss

Warm-stove belly
Wool-skirt hips

Curved and cooking
Warm and wooly

Pretty wife in bright kitchen

Rubbing her belly
Cupping her breasts
Patting her buttocks

Soft arms
Warm rump

BIRDS

Junco
Nuthatch
Chickadee

Red-winged blackbird

Snowy owl
Ruffed grouse

Cardinal
Bluebird

Canada Goose

Hummingbird
Kingfisher

Crow
Magpie

Peregrine falcon

VERACRUZ

Mexico mornings

Tropical seaports
Seaplanes landing

Baskets of angelfish

Tropical streetcars
The music of Spain

Sitting in sunny gardens
On tropical mornings

Looking up from flowers
To palm trees to blue sky

FREIGHT TRAIN

Pennsylvania
New York Central
Great Northern
Union Pacific

Norfolk & Western
Delaware & Hudson
Gulf, Mobile & Ohio
Chicago & North Western
Denver & Rio Grande Western

Rutland

Illinois Central
Baltimore & Ohio
Northern Pacific
Western Pacific

Atlantic Coast Line
Louisville & Nashville
Rock Island Line
Missouri Pacific

Burlington
Boston & Maine

Erie Lackawanna
Lehigh Valley

Southern Pacific
Santa Fe

PAINTER

I

The rainbow-bearded painter

Living on colors

Sits in his sunny studio
And eats his sunny lunch

Belly of colors
Brain of colors

Rainbow-bushed girlfriend

He eats his rainbow salad
And looks upon his paintings

II

Orange crows on black pumpkins
Green girls with red bushes

Mammoths in the Valley of Oaxaca
Moonlight jaguars on jungle beaches

Girl with Cut Throat
Bleeding on Typewriter

Africans with black parachutes
Chinese with yellow parachutes

Helicopter tumbrils
Neon guillotines

Alpine Monks Playing Soccer

Streams of floating skulls
Flocks of burning sheep

Xerxes oryxes
Pelicans skeletons

Naked Schoolgirls Bathing in a Stream

Swallows nesting in ferryboats
Sitting bears with honeypots

Warsaw warscapes

Laboratories of white witches
Halloween parties of homosexual witches

Superdike on her Dikecycle

Snowy owls on black cactus
Junglegyms of naked children

Charwomens picnics
Whorehouse graveyards

Ragged Priest with Drabby Chalice
Wrinkled Rascal on Crinkled Crone

Caravans of cargo dragons
Burning gorillas on motorcycles

Eyeballs in tulips
Crates of children

Pregnant Woman with Broken Back

Mandrills hiding in flowerbeds
Warthogs scowling from wartholes

Rafts of niggers
Bands of robber nuns

Hunchback Moving Among Tombstones

Steam bears and dusty devils
Ruddy ducks and wooly dolphins

Naked girls on zebras
Cities of black glass

Execution of the Flower Thief
Examination of a Slave Girl

Moonlight madmen

Bright-colored tropical dinosaurs
Portraits of tropical whores

SWISS VILLAGE

Sunny side of the Alps

The smell of spring mornings
The form and movement of women

Perfect breasts softly bobbing

Girls lying on the grass in parks
Girls reading books at sidewalk cafes

Pretty girls to the left
Pretty girls to the right

English girls with raincoats
German girls in dirndl skirts

Swedish *fröken*
Dutch *juffrouw*

Spanish *señorita*
Austrian *fräulein*

Italian *signorina*
French *mademoiselle*

SPRING

Visions of mass cunt

All the warm wives
In all the warm beds

Nipple breasts
Navel bellies

Ample tails
Mighty thighs

Coupled couples

Nuns with grass-stained habits
Monks with grass-stained knees

Naughty daughters

Cocky boys
Cunty girls

Working girls with factory lips
Sleek bushes and slippery armpits

Jockstrap cowboys

College girls with glasses
Slipping off their panties

Soft buttocks
Slippery cunts

Hairy halfbacks and cunty coeds
Locked in hot copulation

LOUISIANA

Snapping turtles
Alligator gars

Cypress shadows
Spanish moss

Pirogues

Bayou Black
Bayou Teche

Bayou Boeuf
Bayou Lafourche

Eyes shining in the night

Yellow of raccoons
Green of bullfrogs
Red of alligators
Orange of bears

TRAVELER

I: Winds

Cyclone
Sirocco
Monsoon

Typhoon
Tornado
Chinook

II: Pacific

International seas
International skies

Melting arctic ice
Cooling tropic sand

Red at sunset
Blue in lagoons

Black depths
White surf

III: Africa

Zanzibar
Nairobi
Mombasa

Cairo
Casablanca
Khartoum

IV: Epitaph

Look for the Green Flash
In High Mountains
Tropical Seas
Deserts

ALASKA

Polar hobos

Sleds of salmon
Squaws on swings

Skagway
Sitka
Ketchikan
Kodiak

Jukebox eskimos

Caribou corrals
Caribou cowboys

Seal sandwiches
Puffin pies

Kodiak Island
Brown with bears

Khaki parkas
Khaki kayaks

Eskimo safaris
Polar rodeos

Warm whales

Blubber girls
Blubber bellies

Midnight sun
Midnight rainbows

DEPRESSION

Looking at winter surf

Sinking sun
Iceland gulls

Afternoon of early darkness

The sound of the ocean
White surf on black rocks
The screams of the tide pools

Singing with bleeding lips

MEXICAN STATES

Sonora
Chihuahua
Durango

Guanajuato
Jalisco
Michoacán

Oaxaca
Chiapas
Campéche

Yucatán

ZOO

In the zoological gardens
The gallery of animal art

Cheered by bison bulls
Dolphins and toucans
The shape of penguins

The cat-napping cat
Goose-stepping goose

Dholes in a kraal

Chacma baboons
Anubis baboons

Ursus horribilis

Rocky rams
Peccary pigs

Orange orangs

Mandrills cheeks
Beavers bubbles

Oryx
Kudu
Ibex

Sliding otters
Stamping skunks

African pelicans
Mexican pelicans

Slow loris

Dingo dogs
Congo cats

Shabby bears
Shining seals

TROPICS

I

Green jungle paths

Tropical streams meeting the sea
Surf sounding through rainforest

Jungle beaches
Blue lagoons

Green palms against blue sky
Black palms against red sky

Tropical Trinidad
Sumatra summers

Jamaica-green
Tahiti-green

II

Tropical girls

Red silk on brown skin
Brown girls in white surf

Spicy girls

Sugar girls
Ginger girls
Vanilla girls
Cinnamon girls

Jasmine
Stars
Little brown feet

TITLES

Poems by Wallace Stevens

Sunday Morning
Lions in Sweden

Sailing after Lunch
Connoisseur of Chaos
Girl in a Nightgown

Depression before Spring
Arrival at the Waldorf
Bantams in Pine-Woods

Loneliness in Jersey City
Postcard from the Volcano
Dutch Graves in Bucks County

OFFICE GIRLS

Modern slaves

Shiny pennies for
The crucible city

Blind-alley jobs
Barbed-wire offices

Whitecollar wageslaves
Programmed for defeat

Coffee
Chiclets
Cigarettes

Lost in the whitecollar jungle
Degenerating in treadmill jobs

Crippled voices

Shut off from the sun
Sustained by irrational hopes

Single girls
Surplus cunt

Lonely in the winter city

Straight teeth and crooked minds
Lush bodies and barren souls

Whitecollar daydreams
Television evenings

Rhinestone girls
Chiclet cunts

CALIFORNIA CITIES

Arcadia
Azusa

Bakersfield
Borrego
Brawley

Calexico
Calistoga

Chico
China Lake
Chula Vista

Cotati
Coronado
Coachella

Eureka

Madera
Modesto

Malibu
Mohave
Monterey

Napa
Natoma

Ojai

Palmdale
Pacifica
Placerville

Redwood City

Santee
Sacramento
Sausalito

San Francisco

Shasta
Siskiyou
Sierra City

San Diego

Sonoma
Stockton
Santa Ana

Tecate
Topanga
Torrance

Truckee
Tujunga

Turlock
Torrey Pines

Ukiah

Visalia
Ventura

Yolo

CHANGE

Prophase
Metaphase
Anaphase
Telophase

Sunlight on sunflowers
Moonlight on moonflowers

New rabbits in old foxes
New foxes in old forests
New forests in old valleys

Summer sun and summer days
Winter stars and winter nights

Million-year-old curves
Sixteen-year-old girls

Red sun over green jungle
White moon over black jungle

White face and red whiskers
Red face and white whiskers

Spring-smell
Summer-smell
Autumn-smell
Winter-smell

Ancient slaves with iron collars
Modern slaves with white collars

The red birth
The blue death

Carolina cradle
California coffin

Blue sky and red desert
Red sky and blue desert

Rising over pines
Setting over palms

Freezing void thirty miles up
Molten rock thirty miles down

Green pines against blue sky
Black pines against red sky

Spring green spreading north
Autumn orange spreading south

The smell of the blossom
The taste of the fruit

ANGLO-SAXON STYLE

I

Unprepared for desert-death. Fearing farm-fire,
fondling sow-cow, hearing pig-fart. Order-orgy,
organization-orgy, the surgeon and his life-knife,
reptile-success then reptile-death. South-vision
of gun-mood and night-torches, jail-clang and
death-sweat. Woods-rain and river-rain. No
death-song for this dwarf-death. Night-fires
aid the hunter-killers, swamp-lanterns witness
the mother-murder. Listen to the truncheon-crunch.

II

Photo-poet looking at clown-chalice, battle-song
of the war-whores, sniper-danger then Texas-death.
Tropics-vision, reptile-bright and python-bright.
Zoo-mood, then zoo-visions of cub-fun. Sake-sipping
Japan-man, cunt-crazy, dreaming of safari-rape. Night-worries,
feeling life-pain, desiring death-gift and Asia-grave.
Song-mood to sword-mood, life-smell to death-smell.

III

The night-busy wharf-whores, the day-girls turned
night-dikes, the girl-worker day-slaves, class-trapped,
nice target-tails, afterwards cocktail-jolly, sometimes
champagne-silly. Crash-bang the robot-racket! Old
men preaching nation-danger, vest-assholes talking
pig-price: poet-poison. Birth-luck sings success-song,
his subsidy-sleek lawyer-life. Super-suburban,
super-bourgeois, his trinket-chained whiskey-witch talks
lobby-life and spade-hate. I wish them both beggar-death.

IV

Autumn, stubble-fields pumpkin-bright. Vermont-vision,
woods-snow and snow-walk. Spring-vision, tree-flowers
and brook-sound and meadow-smell. Crescendo-days!
Tiger-life! Free from job-fear, reading of roof-rape
and virgin-murder, pondering the history-mystery,
the day-pain. Food-mood to movie-mood to bed-mood.
Horizon-eyed, knowing river-life and woods-life,
knowing canoe-kiss. Fun-lover, mistake-maker,
cunt-hunter in the cocktail-dark. Lichen-rugged,
science-eyed, dreaming of beach-dawn, then waitress-rape.

MORNING WALK

I

Walking through the morning city

The coffee city

City of popping toasters
City of pretty girls

Whitecollar alarmclocks

New people at every corner
Muscled men and curvy girls

City of lost children

Monday-morning clerks
Full of false hopes

Trucks of cold milk
Trucks of warm bread

Strawberries for the skyscrapers

Black cadillacs and secret taxis
Rising men and sinking men

II

Walking through the morning city
Particle in a puff of smoke

Imagination at the flash point
Ideas bulging in my mind

A set of receptors

The center of the city
Spinning on my neck

All that fine machinery

Reflection in city windows
Shadow on city sidewalks

Student of the city

The fine art of walking
The whirlpool of ideas

The classroom city

LYDIA

Succulent sixteen

Delicious dreamgirl
Young and barefoot

Lollypop lips

Happy voice
Bright face

California-born

Sculptor father
Painter mother

Pink cheeks and tossing hair
Quick mind and flashing eyes

Highschool homework

Bouncing girl
Bobbing breasts

Straining at the bra-strap

Blushing breasts

Whisk-off skirt
Lollypop panties

Baby fat

Small feet
Smooth calves

Breast-kiss
Belly-kiss

Young armpit
New bush

White thighs
Classic cunt

Curvy girl
Creamy girl

Mmmmm!

AMERICAN RIVERS

Alabama
Allegheny
Apalachiola

Brazos

Congaree
Cimarron
Cumberland
Chattahoochee

Chippewa
Cheyenne
Colorado
Columbia

Genesee

Kentucky
Kennebec

Mohawk
Merrimac
Monongahela

Mississippi
Missouri

Niagara

Ohio
Osage

Potomac
Patapsco
Penobscot

Pecos
Platte

Rappahannock

Snake
Seneca
Suwannee

Sabine
Salmon
Santee

Savannah
Shenandoah
Susquehanna

Tugaloo
Tallapoosa
Tallahatchie
Tennessee

GOOD THINGS

White snow
Green pines
Blue sky

Thoreau in Massachusetts
Burroughs in New York
Muir in California

Wild rice
Wild honey
Wild strawberries

Free afternoons
Free mornings
Free nights

The breeze
The skyline
The gulls in the wake

New cities
New friends
New conversations

Poets in San Francisco
Sculptors in Los Angeles
Filmmakers in New York

The smell of grass
The sound of crickets
The sight of stars

BEACH WALK

Muscled men
Curvy girls

Swimming girls with salty bushes
Muscled men with rippled bellies

Michelangelo muscles
Shoulders in the ocean

Girl gymnasts in bikinis

Chinese girls
Jade bikinis

Clambake cats
Salty dogs

Water babies

MANHATTAN

I: Perspective

Primitive man
Primitive city
Primitive society

II: Credo

I, Pedestrian
Employee
Tenant

III: Autumn

October day
Still and overcast

Columns of smoke
Flatten on the clouds

IV: Secretary

White blouse
Crossed legs

Engaged

UNDERLININGS

In my copy of *Ulysses*
By James Joyce

Wedded words

Swanmeat
Moonblue

Cocklepickers
Corpsechewers

Vive le vampire!

Cute as a shithouse rat

Grossbooted draymen
Dullthudding barrels

Brewery barge with export stout

Plovers on toast
Barrel of Bass

Foamborn Aphrodite

Joking Jesus

We are all born in the same way
But we all die in different ways

Pennyweight of powder in a skull

Grandjoker
Archjoker

The scrotum-tightening sea
The cold of interstellar space

Sulphur dung of lions
Old wall where sudden lizards flash

Mr Bloom
Waterlover

Moody brooding
Molly Bloom

Milking Molly into the tea

Monotonous menstruation
Sometimes Molly and Milly together

Weekly carnivals with masked license!
Copulation without population!

Redheaded women buck like goats

Seaside girls
Peachy cheeks

Agreeable females with rich joinctures

Dogsniff

Frisky frumps
Vigorous hips

Suckeress

Mother Grogan
Gummy Granny
Mrs Opisso
Cunty Kate

Nighttown
Sowcunt

CALIFORNIA

Yellow hills
Green oaks

Seacoast ranches

The aroma of eucalyptus
The aroma of chaparral

Redwood beaches
Seacoast flowers

Mustangs in the surf

Driftwood campfires
Moonlight clambakes

Orange blossoms

Pacific palms
Sierra pines

Mohave mornings

Sierra County
Shasta County

Red grapes
Blue grapes
White grapes
Purple grapes

Flower farms

Red roofs
White walls
Green gardens

Bikini beaches

Mountains
Seashore
Desert

PUBLIC PARK

Sitting on a public bench
Enjoying a random afternoon

Public dogs
Public pigeons

Escaped clerks
Girls on the grass
Old men on warm stones
Shady mothers and sunny children

Contemplating my dusty future

Pocketfull of peanuts
Pocketfull of minutes

Sunshine on my skin
Squirrel on my knee

Poetry in my pocket
Melody in my mind

Priceless mood

Alone with my thoughts
On this public planet

Contemplating my mainspring

Watching a magnificent procession
Of public clouds

CHIAPAS

Mexico

Jungle rivers
Blue mountains

Eagles in the morning

Red roofs
White walls
Green gardens

Cantina music

Silver saddles
Black braids

PENSIONER

Urban hermit

Shabby man in old black suit
Ill-fitting suit
Cheap suit

Yellow teeth and yellow nails
Bulging groin and gaping collar

Einstein haircut

Waiting for the newspaper
Looking in bakery windows

Sunday solitaire

Feeble man with baby steps
Smelly man with stubble beard

Hotel winters

Worked at many jobs
Lived in many places

Wornout wageslave
Leftover lifetime

Empty mailbox
Bloody toilets
Parakeet halls
Solitary suppers

Cafeteria Christmas

Ex-acrobat
Ex-sprinter

POLITICAL SLOGANS

Viva Zapata!

Down with charity!
Up with revolution!

Seed the Sahara!

Initiate!
Innovate!

Fill the world with animals!
Fit the cities to the people!

Free movies!
Free foodbars!
Free contraceptives!

Exciting lives!
Mass aristocracy!

Achievement in the mornings!

Free books!
Free plays!
Free music!

Down with privileged families!
Up with natural selection!

Free roller-coasters!
Free encyclopedias!

Koalas for the eucalyptus trees!
Peregrines for the skyscrapers!

Miniskirts!
Bikinis!

Free pies!
Free flowers!
Free motorcycles!

Sunny breakfast tables!

Beach walks!
Woods walks!

Bright kitchens!

Free afternoons!
Free mornings!
Free nights!

Viva!
Viva!
Viva!

NATIONAL PARKS

Big Bend
Bryce Canyon

Crater Lake

Everglades

Glacier
Grand Canyon

Grand Teton
Great Smoky Mountains

Kings Canyon

Mesa Verde
Mount Rainier

Rocky Mountain

Sequoia
Shenandoah

Yellowstone
Yosemite

Zion

STREET

Animal men
Mineral men
Vegetable men

Brooklyn fathers and Oakland mothers
Scullery boys and scabber girls

Academic racketeers
Corporate desperadoes

Pink proles and noble blacks
Crinkled crones and wrinkled rascals

Drugstore cowboys
Cigarstore Indians

Photographers on safari

Movie moguls
Pickle kings

Skyscraper cattlemen
Cattlemens girlfriends

Miami Beach B-girls and Las Vegas V-girls
Freckled *fraus* and speckled *sposas*

Padded shoulders
Padded bras

Beefy-faced butchers
Paper-faced clerks

Dusty farmers and fishy fishermen
Jersey girls and Georgia girls

Pimpled cripples
Polo-clothed men

Communist clowns
Communist cowboys

Dimestore girlfriends

Locomotive husbands
Caboose wives

Diesel dikes and bagel babies
Quality quiffs and common cunts

Chinatown gunmen
Sharkskin suits

Dusty-bushed farmgirls
Shaggy-bushed wolfgirls

Copycat shopkeepers

Schoolgirls in soft sweaters
Teachers in cheap suits

Broken men
Gutted men

Jockeys and boxers
Spades in shades

Rich poets and ragged merchants
Tulsa girls and Tampa girls

Hollywood hookers
Homesick hillbillies

Urban hermits
Manhattan Hamlets

Timid clerks with big-bushed daughters

Salty sailors
Salty girls

Milky-faced milkmen
Sticky-faced piemen

Peoples priests and renegade rabbis
Wooly blacks and silky blondes

Starched nurses
Stainless-steel doctors

Whorehouse handymen

Philosophic plumbers
Boldfaced printers
Big-bellied beermen

College trollops
Jailbait junkies

Shopworn shopgirls
Dumpy frumps

MUSEUM OF MODERN ART

Oil
Casein
Tempera
Polymer

Terra Cotta

Gouache
Gesso

Collage
Assemblage

Welded and Hammered Steel
Brazed with Bronze and Brass

Alfred Jensen
American, born Guatemala
Of Danish parents

Landes Lewitin
American, born Cairo
Of Rumanian parents

Daniel Spoerri
Swiss, born Rumania
Lives in Paris

ZOOK

Boxcar Annie
Old prostitute

Former waitress
Future charwoman

Saddle sores
Crippled voice

Junkie arms
Harlem scars

Much-shaven armpit
Wornout bunghole

Mexican abortions
Bungalow gangbangs

Tattered bush
Chemical cunt

Jail-clang

Waterfront whorehouses
Bordertown brothels

Texas specials

Farmers with dusty peckers
Sailors with salty peckers

Sawdust forearms
Switchblade cheeks

Irish gangsters
Jewish gangsters
Italian gangsters

Fat bellies
Big cigars

Christmas whore
Easter whore

Zook

THE NATIONS

Apache
Arapaho

Chinook
Creek
Commanche

Chippewa
Choctaw
Cherokee
Chickasaw

Delaware
Dakota

Hopi
Kiowa
Mohawk
Navajo

Pima
Paiute
Pueblo
Pawnee

Saginaw
Seneca
Seminole
Sioux

Shoshone
Shawnee

Zuni

POET

Walt Whitman in California
Seaward eyes and windy hair

Lean man in a fat land
Quiet man with quick eyes
Teeming man in a teeming city

Atlantic father
Pacific mother

Bittersweet childhood

Apache man and solo man
Tumbled man and burning man

Night fighter

Manifold man and marathon man
Thriving man and evergreen man

Hopelessly sane

Scrambling man and brooding man
Tommygun man and billygoat man

All components and no resultant
Mixed feelings about everything

Left-wing brain
Right-wing belly

Hooked on oxygen
Hung up on infinity

Microscope days
Telescope nights

A sub-culture of one

Poetry in the morning
Films in the afternoon

Seaport summers

Victory trumpets every day
Every day a jubilee day

Lifetime sundance

Porpoise among flounders
Otter watching lemmings

Street champion

A sense of values
A style of life

USA

Apple valleys

Freight trains
Lake freighters

Red roads in Georgia
Yellow roads in Texas

Indiana summers

The sounds of the trucks
On the interstate highways

Trains crossing rivers

Kansas the Sunflower State
Nevada the Sagebrush State

Pronghorn antelopes

The Pacific Coast
The Gulf Coast

Georgia peaches
Texas mustangs

Footpaths through the redwoods

Beaver valleys
Mountain meadows

Moose feeding in lakes
Desert flowers in bloom

Eagles over Montana

Montana men
Michigan men

Yellowstone wildlife
Everglades wildlife

Orchard planters
Bridge builders

The University of Texas
The University of Colorado

Colorado snowfalls

Burroughs along the Hudson
Muir in the Sierra Nevada

The great Eastern cities
The cities of the Plains
The cities of the West Coast

EXHIBIT NOTES

Hall of North American Mammals
American Museum of Natural History

CANADA LYNX

Mount Albert, Shickshock Range, Gaspe, Quebec

The site of this group is near timber line on the north slope
of Mount Albert . . . The time is late afternoon at the end of
October. A blanket of new-fallen snow . . .

JACK RABBIT

Rancho Tanque Verde, near Tucson, Arizona

This scene shows arid, rocky Arizona at noon in June . . .

WOLF

Gunflint Lake, Minnesota

The time is midnight. The temperature has fallen well below
zero . . .

MULE DEER

Devil's Tower and Belle Fourche River, Wyoming

Southwest up the valley, this October forenoon, meadows are
dotted with cottonwoods and mountain sides are clad with
heavy growths of yellow pine . . . High overhead fracto-cumulus
clouds and feathery wisps of cirrus are seen . . .

BEAVER

Hoister Creek, Gladwin State Game Refuge, Gladwin County, Michigan

It is a still evening in July and the view is to the west, half an hour after sunset . . . The new pond reflects the greenish sky and its pale pink clouds . . .

PORCUPINE

Mount Washington, New Hampshire

The setting for this group is near one of the numerous brooks at the foot of Mount Washington . . . The season is mid-November and the time sunrise. The night clouds are just lifting from the mountain . . .

JAGUAR

Box canyon, near Guaymas, Sonora, Mexico

In this valley behind the coastal ranges and their wreath of fracto-cumulus clouds, illuminated by the setting sun, the dry season is advancing. The month is October . . . Nighthawks, already on the wing . . .

WESTERN GRAY SQUIRREL

Rogue River, southwestern Oregon

The season is the beginning of July and the time about 11 a.m. The view is from the upper branches of a sugar pine looking down into the valley of the Rogue River . . .

BLACK BEAR

A Florida Cypress Swamp

It is hazy Florida weather, the light is pearly, and the time about eight o'clock on a December morning . . .

COTTONTAIL

New York State

October has come . . . the pumpkins are ripe in the cornfield . . .

COYOTE

The Yosemite

The Merced River flows through Bridal Veil Meadows . . . This magnificent view up the Yosemite Valley represents a morning in June . . .

RACCOON

Minnie's Lake, the headwaters of the Suwannee River, in the central part of the Okefenokee Swamp, southeastern Georgia

The time is about midnight in the middle of March . . . The raccoon had come to the water's edge to feed and has just captured a crayfish. The bright star . . . is Vega . . .

GRAY FOX

Great Smoky Mountains National Park, near Gatlinburg, Tennessee

It is late in the afternoon in mid-October at the height of the autumn coloring . . . A red-tailed hawk is soaring across the valley . . .

Printed April 1970 in Santa Barbara by
Noel Young for the Black Sparrow Press.
Design by Barbara Martin. This edition is
limited to 600 copies in paper wrappers,
& 175 copies handbound in boards by
Earle Gray numbered & signed by the poet.

KENNETH GANGEMI was born in 1937 and grew up in Scarsdale, New York. He took an engineering degree at Rensselaer Polytechnic Institute, but for the past eight years has not worked as an engineer. He has lived in various places, but those cities he has lived in longest and knows best are San Francisco, New York, Mexico City, and Los Angeles. His work has appeared in *Art & Literature* and *Transatlantic Review* and his short novel *Olt* was recently published by Calder & Boyars in London and Grossman in New York.